THE QUANTUM LEAP

Breakthrough Decisions for Exponential Growth

CONSULTORIA IA

TO OUR FAMILY

CONTENTS

BRIEF OVERVIEW

In *The Quantum Leap: Breakthrough Decisions for Exponential Growth*, readers are guided through transformative insights and strategies for achieving unprecedented personal and professional growth. This book explores the mindset shifts and strategic choices required to unlock exponential progress, drawing on examples from successful leaders, innovators, and visionaries. Each chapter delves into the key elements that drive breakthrough decisions, including risk-taking, visionary thinking, and resilience. Whether you're an entrepreneur, leader, or anyone seeking profound change, this book provides actionable tools and a clear roadmap for stepping into a new era of possibility.

THREE KEY PROBLEMS THAT THIS BOOK ADDRESSES:

1. **Stagnation in Growth**: Many individuals and organizations reach a plateau where traditional approaches no longer yield significant progress. This book offers strategies to overcome these limitations and move toward exponential growth, breaking free from stagnation and routine.

2. **Fear of Risk and Failure**: Fear of making bold decisions often holds people back from realizing their full potential. *The Quantum Leap* addresses this by providing tools and mindsets to embrace risk intelligently, transform setbacks into learning experiences, and develop resilience.

3. **Lack of a Clear Vision for the Future**: Without a compelling vision, progress often falters. The book guides readers in crafting a visionary roadmap that not only aligns with their goals but also sparks motivation, helping them to visualize and achieve transformative changes.

TARGET AUDIENCE

1. **Entrepreneurs and Business Leaders**: Individuals looking to scale their businesses or drive innovation within their organizations will find strategies for making transformative decisions that lead to exponential growth.

2. **Professionals Seeking Career Advancement**: Those aiming to break through career plateaus or achieve ambitious goals can use the book's insights on vision, resilience, and risk-taking to reach new levels of success.

3. **Self-Improvement Enthusiasts**: People passionate about personal development and mindset growth will find the book valuable for its focus on overcoming fear, building resilience, and embracing change as a path to personal transformation.

4. **Students and Aspiring Innovators**: Young adults and students interested in entrepreneurship, leadership, or high-impact careers can benefit from the guidance on forward-thinking strategies and visionary goal-setting.

PROLOGUE

I n a world defined by rapid change and unprecedented challenges, the difference between incremental progress and exponential growth lies in the decisions we make. *The Quantum Leap* is not just about progress—it's about achieving breakthroughs that reshape our lives, careers, and organizations.

Imagine for a moment the lives of those who seem to move effortlessly from one success to the next, who seize opportunities before they even appear on the horizon, and who, despite setbacks, rise with greater resilience and vision. What makes them different? What secret allows them to make leaps others consider impossible? The answer is not merely in working harder, longer, or even smarter, but in making intentional, decisive choices that carry the potential for massive change.

The Quantum Leap is a journey into this mindset—a blueprint for transforming ambition into impact. This book is designed for the dreamers, the leaders, and the doers, for those who look at their goals and ask, *What more can I do?* It's for anyone ready to break free from the cycle of incremental improvement and aim for something greater, more visionary, and undeniably transformative.

In the following pages, you'll discover not only the practical tools and strategies that underpin exponential growth but also the mindsets that propel it. From cultivating a resilient perspective on failure to crafting a compelling vision that aligns your purpose with action, each chapter is crafted to take you closer to your own quantum leap.

So, if you're ready to defy limitations and accelerate your path to unprecedented success, let's begin. Your quantum leap is waiting.

Theme	Description	Appeal to Readers
Transformative Decision-Making	Guides readers in making high-impact choices that lead to exponential growth rather than incremental progress.	Empowers readers with actionable steps for breakthrough changes in their careers and personal lives.
Resilience and Mindset Shift	Provides strategies to build resilience, embrace failure, and develop a growth-oriented mindset.	Inspires readers to overcome fear, take smart risks, and view setbacks as opportunities for growth.
Visionary Goal Setting	Encourages readers to set ambitious, transformative goals aligned with personal and professional purpose.	Helps readers create a compelling vision and roadmap for achieving remarkable success.

CHAPTER 1: THE POWER OF THE QUANTUM LEAP

In the vast landscape of personal and professional development, there exists a concept so powerful that it can redefine the course of an individual's life or the destiny of a business. This concept is the quantum leap—an explosive, monumental shift that bypasses incremental growth for exponential breakthroughs. It's the kind of growth that transforms good into great, stagnation into acceleration, and limitation into boundless potential. In this first chapter, we will dive deep into the power of the quantum leap, why it is essential for those seeking transformative success, and how harnessing its power requires a unique decision-making approach.

Imagine standing at a precipice, on the edge of two worlds. Behind you is the familiar, with its linear progression and predictable outcomes. Ahead lies the unknown—a realm of boundless opportunities but with no guarantees. Making the leap into this new territory is daunting, to say the least. The unknown is riddled with questions: What if I fail? What if I'm not ready? What if the cost is too high? Yet, those who make the leap and step into this uncertain space often find rewards that exceed their wildest dreams. This is the essence of a quantum leap, a phenomenon where the potential for growth and success expands exponentially.

For decades, people have believed that achieving growth meant following a gradual, step-by-step process. In many ways, society has conditioned us to think that success is slow, requiring years of dedication, sacrifice, and patience. While patience and dedication are indeed valuable, there is another way—one that doesn't play by the same rules. A quantum leap doesn't ask for years of preparation; it demands readiness in the moment. It requires courage to make bold decisions that propel us forward in a matter of days, weeks, or even moments. Instead of walking a path, a quantum leap allows us to sprint ahead on a different path entirely.

What if, rather than thinking of success as a stairway, you considered it a series of gateways? With each quantum leap, a new gateway opens, revealing a whole new level of opportunity. Each leap takes you to a different plane of possibility that might have remained invisible had you taken the linear path. The quantum leap asks us to reframe the way we see risk, growth, and potential, reshaping our goals and our entire perception of success. By understanding and tapping into this power, you're not just aiming to improve; you're aiming to reinvent yourself, your business, and your future.

The Limitations of Incremental Growth

It is easy to feel comfortable with incremental growth. After all, there's a safety net i predictable, step-by-step progress. When we know what the next step looks like, we feel i control. And for most people, control is synonymous with success. Yet, those who achiev groundbreaking success—who create new industries, build empires, and lead revolutior in thought or technology—are not the ones who settled for the predictable. They are th ones who embraced leaps into the unknown, trusting in their ability to adapt, respond, an innovate as they went.

Incremental growth, while comfortable, ultimately limits our potential. Imagine a compan that decides to increase its revenue by 5% every year. Over a decade, the company wi experience a steady, respectable growth. But what if, instead, the company decided t disrupt its market, redefining its strategy to solve a completely different problem or t serve an entirely new audience? Instead of 5% growth, it could be looking at 100% growt or more in a single year. This is not to say that incremental growth is without merit, bu rather to highlight that there are far more powerful possibilities available.

When we rely solely on incremental growth, we allow ourselves to be bound by what w already know. We are, in essence, refining our current state rather than redefining it. W might gain new skills, adopt new technologies, or optimize processes, but these change operate within the same framework. Quantum leaps, on the other hand, take us beyon these limitations. They offer the potential to break free from the constraints of curren knowledge and practices, to go where no path exists and create something entirely new.

Decision-Making for Quantum Leaps

The heart of any quantum leap is the decision to leap itself. Making breakthrough decision: is vastly different from making everyday choices. Breakthrough decisions are characterizec by three main qualities: boldness, clarity, and timing. Without these elements, the decisior to make a quantum leap can easily be lost in doubt or diluted by fear.

Boldness is the courage to make a decision that might defy logic, tradition, or popular opinion. In many cases, quantum leaps don't look practical; they look risky. The key difference is that those who make these leaps don't base their decisions solely on past experiences or probabilities. Instead, they decide based on potential. They are willing tc make the leap before they know exactly how things will unfold. This is not reckless; it's calculated risk-taking, fueled by a strong belief in the potential for transformative growth.

Clarity is equally essential. Clarity doesn't mean that you have every answer before you leap; rather, it means you have a vision so clear that you're willing to take the leap, knowing that every challenge you encounter will ultimately bring you closer to that vision This kind of clarity allows you to focus on the opportunity rather than the obstacles. When you're clear about what you want, your decisions naturally align with your goals, making the path toward quantum growth a direct one.

inally, there's timing. Quantum leaps happen not only because of boldness and clarity but ecause of a keen sense of timing. Recognizing the right moment to make a move is critical. Often, this timing isn't about waiting for perfect conditions but about knowing when to act decisively. In many cases, those who achieve extraordinary success do so because they ecognize windows of opportunity that others overlook. These windows are often brief and an close just as quickly as they open, which is why decisive action is key.

Building a Mindset for Exponential Growth

At the core of quantum leaps lies a mindset of exponential growth—a way of thinking that goes beyond limitations, challenges, and fears. To take a quantum leap, you must cultivate a mindset that not only welcomes rapid growth but expects it. This means stepping into a mental space where growth becomes the default, not the exception. Such a mindset transforms obstacles into stepping stones, allowing you to view every challenge as an opportunity for acceleration.

One of the most powerful elements of this mindset is the belief that there are no true limits to your potential. Belief may sound simplistic, but it is a profound force. The way you perceive your capabilities and opportunities directly influences the decisions you make and the actions you take. People who make quantum leaps often share a deep, unwavering belief in their ability to achieve the extraordinary. This belief fuels their resilience, allowing them to persist when others give up. By adopting this mindset, you set yourself up to notice and seize opportunities for quantum growth.

In contrast, a fixed mindset creates invisible barriers. It tells you to be cautious, to stay within the realm of what's "realistic" or "achievable." But a growth mindset, especially one focused on exponential growth, pushes you to see beyond these boundaries. It encourages you to question assumptions, challenge norms, and reimagine possibilities. In doing so, it sets the stage for transformative success.

Case Studies: The Quantum Leap in Action

To understand the real-world power of the quantum leap, let's consider a few examples of people and organizations who harnessed this approach to achieve extraordinary results. Each of these examples highlights how a bold decision, rooted in a mindset of exponential growth, created seismic shifts that transformed entire industries.

Take, for instance, Apple's decision to enter the mobile phone market. At the time, Apple was known for its computers and had little experience in telecommunications. Yet, with the launch of the iPhone, the company made a quantum leap that redefined not only its brand but also the future of mobile technology. Apple didn't simply make a better phone; it created a new product category, an ecosystem, and a customer experience that would revolutionize the industry. The iPhone was a result of breakthrough decision-making, executed at the right moment with a bold vision.

Another example is Netflix, which started as a DVD rental service. Rather than competing incrementally within the rental market, Netflix made a quantum leap by pivoting into streaming. This decision, although risky, positioned Netflix as a pioneer in digital content and forever changed the way we consume media. By being willing to disrupt its own business model, Netflix set itself up for exponential growth that would see it become a global entertainment giant.

These examples show that quantum leaps are not random. They are the result of intentional, bold decision-making, fueled by a belief in the potential for transformative growth. By choosing to leap rather than step, these companies didn't just keep up with the market; they reshaped it.

Embracing the Leap: Your Path to Exponential Growth

As you stand on the edge of your own quantum leap, you must ask yourself: Am I willing to leave behind the comfort of incremental progress for the possibility of extraordinary growth? Embracing a quantum leap is a choice to go beyond what's comfortable, what's known, and what's predictable. It's a decision to pursue a vision so compelling that it pulls you forward, even when the outcome isn't guaranteed.

Taking a quantum leap isn't about eliminating fear; it's about taking action despite it. The road ahead may be uncertain, and challenges are inevitable, but those who leap know that every step is bringing them closer to something monumental. Each decision, each risk, each bold move compounds, creating a force of momentum that drives exponential growth.

In the chapters that follow, we'll explore practical tools and strategies to help you make these breakthrough decisions. We'll dive into the psychology of high-stakes decision-making, learn how to leverage intuition and analysis, and uncover methods to navigate risk with confidence. This is your invitation to step into the unknown, to harness the power of the quantum leap, and to redefine what's possible in your life and career.

In the quest for exponential growth, the bold and decisive act of taking a quantum leap can lead to profound success, yet it also carries the risk of failure. While the allure of rapid transformation is compelling, not every leap leads to the desired outcome. Successes show us what's possible when we embrace a mindset of growth and act decisively, while failures remind us of the importance of strategic timing, readiness, and a clear vision. In this chapter, we will dive into two in-depth case studies: one of success and one of failure. By examining each, we aim to uncover the patterns, decisions, and lessons that can guide us toward making more informed quantum leaps in our own pursuits.

Case Study 1: The Quantum Leap of Amazon Prime — A Case of Exponential Success

To understand the potential for a quantum leap to propel a company forward, we need only look at Amazon and its launch of Amazon Prime. By 2005, Amazon had already established itself as a leading e-commerce platform, but the company faced the challenge of differentiating itself in an increasingly competitive market. Competitors like eBay were growing rapidly, and other big players were beginning to see the potential in online retail. Jeff Bezos, Amazon's CEO, understood that to secure Amazon's dominance, the company needed more than incremental improvements. It needed a radical shift — a quantum leap.

Amazon Prime: A Leap Beyond Conventional E-Commerce

The idea behind Amazon Prime was deceptively simple: charge customers an annual fee for unlimited, fast shipping on thousands of items. However, beneath the simplicity of the concept lay a bold and innovative business strategy with exponential potential. When Amazon Prime launched in 2005, it was priced at $79 per year and offered two-day shipping on eligible purchases. For many, the idea of paying a yearly subscription for shipping seemed risky. Would customers find enough value in the membership to justify the cost? Would the free shipping eat into Amazon's margins?

Despite these questions, Amazon pressed forward, launching Prime with a vision that extended beyond immediate profit. The goal was not only to drive sales but to reshape customer behavior. By removing the friction associated with shipping costs, Amazon aimed to increase purchase frequency, cultivate loyalty, and transform Prime members into repeat customers.

The Numbers: Amazon Prime's Impact on Growth

The results of this leap were nothing short of remarkable. Within just a few years, Prime members were shown to spend **over twice as much** on Amazon compared to non-members, averaging around $1,500 annually compared to $625 by non-members. With each passing year, the membership base grew, and so did Amazon's market dominance. By 2023, Amazon Prime boasted over **200 million subscribers worldwide**, an astonishing achievement that demonstrates the impact of a well-timed, bold decision.

From a revenue perspective, Prime was transformative. In 2022, Amazon's revenue from Prime subscriptions alone reached **$31.8 billion**, making it a critical part of Amazon's income stream. Additionally, Prime members' increased spending across other Amazon services, like Amazon Fresh, Amazon Video, and even the company's physical retail stores, highlights how the initial leap to launch Prime created a ripple effect across Amazon's entire ecosystem. This quantum leap not only accelerated Amazon's growth but fundamentally changed the way we think about retail and loyalty programs.

Lessons Learned from Amazon Prime's Success

1. **Customer-Centric Vision:** Amazon Prime succeeded because it focused on creating value for the customer, not just short-term gains. Prime redefined customer loyalty and created a powerful ecosystem where customers were motivated to stay engaged with the brand.

2. **Commitment to Scale:** Amazon Prime was not an experiment; it was a long-term commitment. Bezos and his team were willing to sustain losses in shipping to create a powerful competitive advantage.

3. **Timing and Readiness:** Amazon's decision to launch Prime was timed perfectl within the context of growing e-commerce and consumer demand fo convenience. This leap was taken with the right market conditions in place.

Through Amazon Prime, Amazon showed the world how a quantum leap could yiel exponential growth. However, while Amazon's story is inspiring, not every leap turns ou this way. The next example underscores the importance of careful planning and alignmen with market readiness before making the leap.

Case Study 2: Quibi — A Quantum Leap to Nowhere

In contrast to Amazon's success, the story of Quibi offers a cautionary tale about the risk associated with quantum leaps that may be mistimed or misaligned with market needs Founded by media mogul Jeffrey Katzenberg and former HP CEO Meg Whitman, Quibi wa a streaming platform designed to deliver "quick bites" of content: short episodes meant tc be watched on mobile devices. Quibi's bold vision was to create a new category o streaming content, targeting on-the-go viewers who might only have a few minutes tc watch.

With a massive **$1.75 billion** investment in funding, Quibi had everything it needed tc make a splash in the entertainment industry — except for timing and alignment with consumer demand.

The Vision Behind Quibi

Katzenberg and Whitman believed they had identified a gap in the market. The premise was that today's fast-paced world would welcome ultra-short videos that provided quality entertainment in a format that fit into the cracks of busy schedules. Quibi's technology allowed users to seamlessly switch between portrait and landscape mode, a novel feature for video streaming at the time. The platform launched in April 2020, just as the COVID-19 pandemic was altering the way people consumed media.

Despite their ambitious vision and substantial funding, Quibi failed to gain traction. Within six months of launch, it became apparent that the platform was struggling. By October 2020, Quibi announced it would shut down, returning the remaining funds to investors and laying off its staff. The question remains: *What went wrong with Quibi's quantum leap?*

The Numbers: Quibi's Rapid Decline

Quibi's short-lived journey paints a clear picture of the perils of a misaligned quantum leap. Despite raising nearly $2 billion, Quibi only managed to attract **500,000 subscribers**, far below the millions it had projected. The company had anticipated a large audience willing to pay $4.99 per month with ads or $7.99 without ads. But by October 2020, just six months after launch, Quibi's financial losses were significant, and its audience was dwindling. The decision to shut down followed reports of disappointing viewership and a bleak future for the platform.

Key Reasons for Quibi's Failure

1. **Misaligned Market Demand:** While Quibi's founders envisioned an audience eager for "quick bites" of content, the market was not receptive. The pandemic meant people were more at home, looking for longer-form content, a stark contrast to Quibi's mobile-first, short-episode format.

2. **High Pricing and Low Value Perception:** Unlike Amazon Prime, which offered substantial value, Quibi's offering seemed limited and costly. Viewers found little motivation to pay for a service that didn't provide the breadth of content available on platforms like Netflix or Disney+.

3. **Competition and Differentiation:** Quibi entered an already saturated streaming market without offering enough differentiation to justify its cost. The platform's unique selling point, the ability to watch short-form, vertical content, wasn't compelling enough to shift consumer behavior.

4. **Costly Content Investments:** Quibi invested heavily in content, enlisting big-name celebrities and high production values. However, this focus on big-budget content proved unsustainable when the subscriber base didn't meet expectations, leading to high burn rates with little return.

Lessons Learned from Quibi's Failure

1. **Understand Market Readiness:** Quibi's timing did not align with the market's needs. A successful quantum leap requires an environment that is ready to embrace the change being offered.

2. **Value Proposition Alignment:** In any quantum leap, the value provided must be clear and compelling. Customers must feel that what they are paying for brings unique benefits they cannot find elsewhere.

3. **Differentiation and Sustainability:** A leap into a competitive market requires a unique offering that stands out. Quibi's lack of true differentiation made it difficult to compete with established players.

4. **Effective Risk Assessment:** Even with substantial funding, risks must be evaluated. Quantum leaps require calculated risks, not just financial investment but alignment with market trends and behaviors.

Reflection: Which Path Will You Choose?

The stories of Amazon Prime and Quibi provide us with valuable insights into the nature of quantum leaps. Both companies made bold decisions, but while Amazon succeeded in redefining consumer behavior and achieving exponential growth, Quibi's failure underscores the need for careful evaluation before making the leap.

For those considering their own quantum leap, the lessons are clear: it is essential to have a customer-centric approach, to align with market demand, and to ensure that the timing and resources support sustainable growth. By taking calculated risks, we can maximize the potential of our quantum leaps and minimize the chance of falling short. So, as you think about your next big move, consider the following questions:

1. Is there a strong market demand for the leap I'm about to make?
2. Am I willing to sustain initial losses or challenges to achieve long-term rewards?
3. How does my vision align with my customers' needs, and how will this leap improve their experience?
4. Is the market ready for this change, or am I too early or too late to capitalize on the opportunity?

Summary Table of Key Statistics and Insights

Factor	Amazon Prime (Success)	Quibi (Failure)
Launch Date	2005	2020
Initial Funding	Internal Amazon funds	$1.75 billion
Subscribers	200 million by 2023	500,000 within 6 months
Annual Revenue (2022)	$31.8 billion	N/A (company closed)
Value Proposition	Unlimited, fast shipping, exclusive content	Short-form, mobile-first video content
Customer Spending (Annual)	Prime: ~$1,500; Non-Prime: ~$625	Insufficient to support business model
Primary Lesson	Customer-centric vision with clear value	Misaligned with market needs and timing

Both of these cases offer powerful lessons. Amazon Prime's journey underscores the importance of a compelling, customer-focused value proposition and a willingness to take calculated risks for long-term gain. Quibi's story, in contrast, warns against taking leaps without thorough alignment with market demand, differentiation, and clear, sustainable value for the consumer.

As you consider your own quantum leap, keep these principles in mind. Every leap involves risk, but by grounding your decisions in strategy, timing, and market alignment, you can increase your chances of making a successful quantum leap and achieving exponential growth.

CHAPTER 2: EMBRACING THE UNKNOWN – CHARTING THE PATH TO QUANTUM GROWTH

Quantum growth is not for the faint-hearted. It's the realm of the ambitious, those who dare to dream beyond the conventional and are willing to venture into the unknown. Imagine yourself at the edge of a vast, unexplored frontier. It's daunting, yes, but exhilarating. And the truth is, this is where exponential growth lies—not in the predictable or the safe, but in the places few dare to tread.

But what does it take to cultivate this level of growth? In this chapter, we'll dive into the often-overlooked, deeper, foundational shifts that must happen within you before you can experience true, exponential success. You'll face challenges, of course, but each one can be a stepping stone to massive breakthroughs. Remember, the reward lies in the risk, in the leaps you're brave enough to take.

Defining Your Quantum Leap – More Than Just Big Goals

Let's start with an idea that might challenge you: if your goals don't scare you, they're not big enough. It sounds almost cliché, doesn't it? Yet, if you're serious about exponential growth, you must stretch beyond comfort zones and redefine what's possible. Think about a goal you currently have in mind. Does it excite you? Does it challenge you? If it doesn't, then it's likely still operating within the realm of incremental growth—where results are predictable, but rewards are also limited.

Now, try imagining what your life or business would look like if you removed the mental barriers you've set around yourself. Picture your wildest vision of success, no matter how improbable it feels. Write it down. Yes, right now. Describe it in detail. What does this future look like? How does it feel? This is your starting point—a benchmark for your quantum leap. Remember, achieving quantum growth requires clarity in vision, even if you don't have all the answers on how to get there yet. And this vision must be bold enough to challenge the very limits you've previously set for yourself.

Challenge 1 for Future Growth: Embracing Radical Vision

It's tempting to set goals that feel attainable; we crave certainty, and the brain loves the security of the known. But settling for what's feasible won't get you where you truly want to be. True breakthrough ideas exist in a place of uncertainty, beyond what you already know.

Ask yourself: What does a wildly ambitious version of success look like? Write it down, visualize it, make it vivid. Define the version of you who would dare to go after this dream. Commit to creating a vision that is clear yet challenging, something that fuels your ambition and pushes you to think exponentially, not linearly.

Rewriting Your Mental Blueprint – The Power of Perspective

Quantum growth is as much an inner journey as it is an external one. Most people fail to grow exponentially not because they lack resources or ambition but because they're operating from old mental frameworks—ones that have been shaped by past experiences, self-doubt, and society's limitations. It's like trying to run new, complex software on an outdated operating system. It simply won't work.

To truly leap forward, you need to rewrite your mental blueprint. This involves questioning assumptions, redefining beliefs, and ultimately changing the way you see yourself and the world around you. Take a moment to reflect on your current beliefs about success. Are they empowering, or are they limiting? Consider the stories you tell yourself about what's possible. The most successful people often embrace beliefs that others consider 'unrealistic.' They don't see limitations; they see opportunities.

Challenge 2 for Future Growth: Updating Your Belief System

Ask yourself: What beliefs are currently holding me back from quantum growth? Identify at least three limiting beliefs you hold. Write them down, and then, beside each one, write a new, empowering belief that supports your exponential vision. This shift in mindset is essential, as it will serve as the foundation for every bold action you take.

Consider this exercise as ongoing. As you grow, revisit your beliefs, challenge them, and refine them. Quantum growth demands constant evolution, not only in actions but in thought.

Taking Calculated Risks – Stepping Into Discomfort

Many people fear risk, equating it with recklessness. But quantum growth requires a unique perspective on risk—a willingness to embrace uncertainty in the pursuit of something extraordinary. In fact, you could argue that taking calculated risks is the only way to achieve exponential success. Consider a decision you've been hesitating to make, perhaps because it feels too risky or uncertain. What if you reframed it, not as a risk but as a strategic move toward your vision? This is where growth lives, just beyond the borders of your comfort zone.

Now, this doesn't mean leaping blindly. Calculated risk involves a blend of intuition, preparation, and analysis. To grow exponentially, you must develop an ability to evaluate risk and act decisively, understanding that growth and certainty rarely coexist. The most successful people master the art of betting on themselves even when the odds seem impossible.

Challenge 3 for Future Growth: Cultivating a Bold Relationship with Risk

Think of a bold decision you've been avoiding, perhaps due to the perceived risk. Reflect on what you truly have to lose versus what you stand to gain. Ask yourself: What's the best-case scenario if I succeed, and what's the worst-case scenario if I don't? Quantum growth is about understanding that the upside often outweighs the downside—and having the courage to act on it.

Begin with small steps if needed. Take a calculated risk this week. Experience the discomfort, but more importantly, notice the growth that follows. This is the pathway to

uilding your tolerance for uncertainty, a crucial trait in those who achieve quantum
uccess.

Building a Network for Exponential Influence – The Power of Relationships

You may be familiar with the saying, "You are the average of the five people you spend the
most time with." While this might sound simple, it's a profound truth for those seeking
exponential growth. The people you surround yourself with can either propel you forward
or keep you stagnant. Quantum growth demands a supportive, ambitious network—a circle
of people who inspire you to think bigger, act bolder, and stay accountable to your vision.

Ask yourself: Are the people around me supporting or stalling my growth? Who challenges
me to think bigger? Who believes in my vision? Remember, exponential growth often
requires partnerships, collaborations, and mentors who are already where you want to be.
Building this network is a process that involves intention and strategy. Seek out those who
share your vision or have accomplished what you aspire to achieve.

Challenge 4 for Future Growth: Cultivating a Powerful Network

Start identifying people you admire, mentors, or even peers who can offer guidance and
insight. Reach out, attend events, join masterminds—take action to build meaningful
connections. Choose individuals who inspire and challenge you, those who push you to
think outside the box and aim for exponential growth.

This isn't just about gaining advice; it's about fostering relationships that nurture and
elevate you. Commit to connecting with one person each week who aligns with your vision.
Over time, this network will not only support your growth but may also provide unforeseen
opportunities.

Embracing Resilience – Navigating Setbacks with a Growth Mindset

Every journey toward quantum growth will face setbacks. Failures are not only inevitable
but necessary. They offer valuable lessons that no amount of planning or preparation can
provide. But here's the critical difference between those who achieve exponential success
and those who don't: resilience. Those who achieve quantum growth see setbacks not as
failures but as feedback—a necessary component of learning and refinement.

Resilience is about building the ability to bounce back, adapt, and continue moving forward
despite obstacles. It's about developing a mindset that views challenges as stepping stones
rather than roadblocks. Each time you encounter a challenge, you're given the chance to
learn, adapt, and come back stronger.

Challenge 5 for Future Growth: Developing Resilience in the Face of Setbacks

Think back to a recent setback or challenge. How did you respond? Did you view it as a
failure, or did you extract valuable lessons from the experience? Make a habit of
documenting your challenges and the lessons you learn from each one. Reframe setbacks as
necessary steps in the journey toward quantum growth.

Practice resilience by embracing challenges, viewing them as opportunities to test and
refine your approach. Each setback is a lesson and a building block for future growth. Make
resilience a cornerstone of your strategy.

Stepping Boldly into the Future

This journey toward quantum growth will be filled with challenges, but it will also be deeply rewarding. As you cultivate a vision that excites and challenges you, as you rewrite limiting beliefs and embrace risk, build a powerful network, and develop resilience, you'll discover a new level of personal and professional growth that you may have previously thought impossible.

Quantum growth is not a path for everyone. It demands courage, perseverance, and a relentless belief in your ability to achieve the extraordinary. But for those who dare to embrace it, the rewards are profound. You'll not only transform your own life but, potentially, the lives of those around you. So, as you close this chapter, make a commitment to yourself. Decide that from this point forward, you will think bigger, act bolder, and strive for the exponential growth that lies just beyond the boundaries of your current reality.

Key Concept	Description	Challenge for Growth	Action Step
Radical Vision	Setting an ambitious, even intimidating, vision that surpasses comfort zones.	Create a bold, vivid vision that excites and challenges current limits.	Define an inspiring, detailed vision that promotes exponential thinking.
Belief System Rewrite	Changing limiting beliefs to enable mental growth aligned with ambitious goals.	Identify and replace at least three limiting beliefs with empowering ones.	Regularly reflect and update beliefs to support exponential goals.
Calculated Risk	Embracing uncertainty and calculated risks to drive exponential progress.	Assess a decision you've been avoiding due to risk and reframe it as a growth step.	Take a calculated risk weekly to increase resilience to uncertainty.
Powerful Network	Building relationships that encourage bold thinking and support growth.	Connect with individuals who challenge, inspire, and align with your vision.	Reach out to one new person weekly to build a network for exponential influence.
Resilience Development	Adopting a mindset that sees setbacks as lessons rather than failures.	Reflect on past setbacks, extract lessons, and strengthen resilience.	Document challenges and lessons learned; reframe failures as growth steps.

In the journey to quantum growth, there comes a defining point where innovators must step beyond the familiar, leaving behind the predictable and comfortable strategies that lead only to incremental progress. Instead, they choose to venture into the unknown, where groundbreaking ideas, transformative technologies, and exponential leaps are born. What separates those who make these leaps from those who remain grounded in safety? In this chapter, we'll delve into the mindset and attitudes that empowered some of the greatest innovators of recent times to face and ultimately transcend daunting challenges.

hrough their perspectives, we can glean invaluable lessons on embracing the unknown
nd charting a path to quantum growth.

Bold Curiosity: The Willingness to Ask "What If?"

t the heart of every quantum leap is a powerful question: *What if?* Innovators like Steve
obs, Elon Musk, and Jeff Bezos exemplified the radical curiosity that propelled them
eyond known boundaries. Each embraced an unrelenting desire to explore possibilities, to
sk questions that defied the conventions of their industries. Steve Jobs, for example,
onsistently challenged the status quo, asking why computers had to look and feel the way
ley did in the 1980s. He questioned the very concept of how technology should interact
ith humans, leading to a legacy of products that would eventually reshape entire
ndustries.

his kind of curiosity is more than just intellectual; it's an embodied willingness to *see
eyond the present limitations*, one that demands an open mind and an appetite for risks. It
sks the individual to suspend disbelief and imagine, if only for a moment, what could exist
the rules were redefined. As a reader, ask yourself: When was the last time you
uestioned the assumptions that govern your work or life? How often do you entertain the
eemingly impossible? Curiosity, as exemplified by these innovators, isn't a passive state
ut an active, persistent choice to look at things as if you're seeing them for the first time.
his outlook is essential to charting a path toward exponential growth.

Embracing Failure as a Learning Process

Most people view failure as a setback, a sign to turn back, but for the pioneers of quantum
rowth, failure is simply part of the journey. Thomas Edison's famous statement, "I have
ot failed. I've just found 10,000 ways that won't work," perfectly encapsulates this
nindset. Each "failure" is an invaluable lesson that brings you closer to a solution, a
tepping stone in the journey toward breakthrough discoveries. Elon Musk's ventures into
pace exploration, electric vehicles, and even brain-computer interfaces (through
Neuralink) are rife with initial failures that would deter most people. But Musk's
villingness to embrace these failures as learning opportunities rather than deterrents
llustrates a vital trait for anyone aiming for exponential growth.

f you are on a similar journey, it's essential to recalibrate how you perceive failure. Rather
han seeing it as a signal to quit, understand that failure is an instructor, a necessary
xperience that adds depth to your knowledge and capabilities. This acceptance can free
ou from the fear of making mistakes, liberating you to explore more daring,
ransformative avenues. In your own journey, ask yourself: Are you willing to fail—and
ven to fail repeatedly—if it means getting closer to a monumental breakthrough? The
esson here is that those who achieve quantum growth do not fear failure but instead
velcome it as an inevitable and essential part of their journey.

3. A Relentless Drive for Mastery

While curiosity and a willingness to fail are important, they must be matched by a
relentless pursuit of mastery. True innovators understand that superficial knowledge isn't
enough to bring about exponential change. To truly disrupt an industry, you need to dig
deeper, understanding its intricacies, knowing where weaknesses lie, and gaining insights
that allow for transformation. Jeff Bezos exemplified this commitment to mastery. His

obsessive focus on operational efficiency, customer satisfaction, and logistics transformed Amazon from an online bookstore to a global titan, pioneering e-commerce and cloud computing.

Mastery demands more than a passing interest; it requires intense focus, study, and often a deep-seated love for the subject. When you look at your own work, ask yourself: Are you willing to put in the time to become not just good, but exceptional? Quantum growth requires not only breadth but depth—an in-depth understanding that allows you to spot opportunities and leverage them in ways others cannot. Bezos, Jobs, and Musk invested countless hours honing their understanding of the sectors they entered. This dedication is often what separates fleeting success from transformative innovation.

4. The Courage to Challenge the Status Quo

A defining characteristic of innovators who achieve quantum leaps is a refusal to accept "the way things are." They possess a unique courage that enables them to confront and often dismantle existing paradigms. One powerful example is how Uber disrupted the traditional taxi industry. Travis Kalanick and Garrett Camp saw an opportunity to challenge an industry steeped in rigid regulations, limited customer service, and monopolistic tendencies. Uber's innovation didn't just change transportation—it shifted consumer expectations and sparked a ripple effect across multiple industries.

Challenging the status quo often means going against public opinion, industry norms, and even legal constraints. It's a daunting path that requires resilience, clarity of purpose, and an unwavering belief in one's vision. Think about your own industry or organization. Are there practices and conventions that you feel could be improved or overturned? Taking a stance against the established order is not easy, and it may invite criticism or resistance, but those who chart a path to exponential growth understand that change rarely occurs within comfort zones. To disrupt, you must first be willing to dissent.

5. Leveraging Technology as a Tool for Transformation

For today's most impactful innovators, technology is not merely a tool; it is the medium through which they envision and execute their groundbreaking ideas. In recent years, technological advancement has opened unprecedented possibilities, from artificial intelligence and robotics to genetic engineering and quantum computing. Take the case of Larry Page and Sergey Brin, who used technology not just to build a better search engine but to revolutionize the way information is accessed and organized globally. Their approach to leveraging machine learning, AI, and data processing has not only transformed Google but has redefined our relationship with information.

For those looking to make quantum leaps, technology offers an ever-expanding toolkit. However, it's essential to remember that technology itself is not the end goal; rather, it is a means of realizing a vision. As you approach your own challenges, consider: Are you fully harnessing the potential of available technologies? Are you willing to explore emerging technologies that could amplify your impact? Innovators who achieve quantum growth understand that technology is the vessel through which vision takes form, but it is their purpose and insight that steer it.

. Building a Culture of Risk-Taking and Resilience

No innovator operates in a vacuum; the greatest leaps happen in environments that cultivate and reward risk-taking. Leaders like Elon Musk and Reed Hastings (of Netflix) created cultures within their companies that foster resilience and encourage their teams to take calculated risks. For Musk, this meant establishing a work environment at SpaceX that didn't penalize failure but instead sought to learn from it. For Hastings, it meant building Netflix into a company where bold, unconventional decisions were encouraged, even if they resulted in initial setbacks.

Creating this kind of culture is essential for organizations aiming for quantum growth. Teams need the psychological safety to experiment without fear, knowing they have the support of leadership. Without this foundation, innovative ideas are stifled, and progress is limited to incremental changes. As a leader or a member of a team, consider whether you are contributing to a culture that values exploration and resilience. Are you encouraging those around you to take risks, or are you bound by a culture that prioritizes safety over progress? For quantum growth, you must foster an environment that allows for bold experimentation and the tenacity to recover from inevitable missteps.

7. A Deep Commitment to Purpose and Impact

Purpose is the invisible force driving the world's greatest innovators. For individuals like Elon Musk, purpose is not just a mission statement; it's a vision that fuels every decision, every project, and every setback along the way. Musk's purpose—to make life multi-planetary—has guided his efforts in space exploration, renewable energy, and AI. This clarity of purpose has not only inspired his teams but has drawn in investors, customers, and fans who share or admire that vision.

When you have a deep commitment to purpose, it's easier to endure the challenges and uncertainties that accompany exponential growth. In your own journey, reflect on your purpose. Are you working toward a vision that excites and motivates you? Purpose anchors innovators, giving them the endurance to push through barriers that would deter others. Those who seek quantum growth must find a purpose that fuels their resilience and inspires those around them.

8. Adaptability and Openness to Pivot

Finally, those who achieve quantum leaps understand that the path to growth is rarely a straight line. The willingness to pivot—sometimes drastically—is essential. Consider the case of Slack, which began as an internal communication tool for a gaming company. When the gaming concept didn't take off, founder Stewart Butterfield had the insight and flexibility to pivot to a communication platform, a decision that led to Slack becoming one of the world's most popular workplace tools.

Adaptability means being open to changing your approach, even if it means abandoning ideas you've invested time and resources in. Innovators understand that flexibility can be the difference between stagnation and breakthrough. As you work towards your goals, consider: Are you willing to pivot if new opportunities or challenges emerge? Quantum growth demands an openness to adaptation, knowing that your ultimate destination may require several unexpected turns along the way.

Charting Your Own Path to Quantum Growth

The attitudes of history's greatest innovators are not reserved for a select few; they are qualities that any dedicated individual or organization can adopt. To embrace the unknown and chart a path to quantum growth, one must be relentlessly curious, willing to face and learn from failure, dedicated to mastery, brave enough to challenge norms, and capable of leveraging technology as a transformative tool. Equally, building a culture that supports risk-taking, aligning with a deep purpose, and remaining adaptable are indispensable attitudes for anyone looking to make a transformative impact.

As you continue your journey, remember that quantum growth is not about incremental steps but about a fundamental shift in perspective, strategy, and courage. By embodying these attitudes, you too can embrace the unknown, paving the way for breakthroughs that extend beyond the imaginable and into the realm of exponential impact.

CHAPTER 3: THE BLUEPRINT OF EXPONENTIAL GROWTH - MODELS TO MEASURE AND SCALE BREAKTHROUGHS

A chieving exponential growth demands more than incremental improvements; it requires a paradigm shift in the way we think, decide, and measure our progress. This chapter explores three essential models that form the backbone of making breakthrough decisions. Through these models, you will learn how to project growth, assess risk, and set up sustainable scaling strategies that push your growth trajectory from linear to exponential. Each model is underpinned by mathematical formulas and practical applications, allowing you to visualize, measure, and optimize for sustained quantum leaps in growth.

1. THE EXPONENTIAL GROWTH PROJECTION MODEL (EGPM)

In the initial stages of any ambitious endeavor, one of the most critical steps is projecting growth. Unlike traditional models that assume steady, linear increases, the Exponential Growth Projection Model (EGPM) is designed to account for the rapid, compounding effect that often accompanies innovative, high-impact strategies.

Core Concept: Compounded Growth

At the heart of EGPM is the principle of compounded growth. Imagine a snowball rolling down a hill—small at first, it gains size and speed, picking up more snow as it goes. This is compounded growth in action, where each round of growth builds upon the last. To predict this growth effectively, the model uses the following formula:

$$G = P \times (1 + r)^t$$

Where:

- **GGG** = Projected growth value after a given time period
- **PPP** = Initial value or starting point (e.g., initial revenue or user base)
- **rrr** = Growth rate per period (as a decimal)
- **ttt** = Number of time periods

For example, let's say your company's user base starts at 1,000 users, and you anticipate a growth rate of 15% per month. Over a 12-month period, using the formula, we can project

$$G = 1000 \times (1 + 0.15)^{12} = 1000 \times 5.35 = 5,350$$

the user base as follows:

This model reveals the compounding power of a 15% growth rate. Within a year, a mere 15% monthly increase transforms 1,000 users into over 5,000.

Application and Analysis

EGPM is most useful for long-term goal-setting. By understanding the mathematical impact of compounded growth, decision-makers can set realistic yet ambitious targets. However, bear in mind that exponential growth requires constant innovation, customer engagement, and market adaptability. This model should be periodically revisited, with growth rates adjusted based on actual performance and market shifts. EGPM can guide you through the planning phases of a new initiative or when launching a breakthrough product, providing a powerful tool to visualize potential future impact.

2. THE RISK-RETURN ANALYSIS MODEL (RRAM)

igh-impact, exponential decisions carry a significant element of risk. The Risk-Return nalysis Model (RRAM) offers a balanced approach to quantify and manage this risk in ursuit of exponential growth. By framing risk in terms of potential return, RRAM allows ou to evaluate whether the rewards of a high-stakes decision justify the potential ownsides.

ore Concept: Risk-Adjusted Return

RAM leverages the concept of risk-adjusted return, which adjusts growth projections

$$RRA = E(R) - \frac{\sigma^2}{2}$$

ased on the likelihood of various risks. A widely used formula in this model is:

Vhere:

- **RRARRARRA** = Risk-adjusted return on investment
- **E(R)E(R)E(R)** = Expected return without risk adjustment
- σ\sigma$\sigma$ = Standard deviation of return (a measure of risk volatility)

et's break this down with an example. Imagine a startup projecting a return of 30% (E(R) = 0.30) on a breakthrough marketing campaign. However, due to market volatility, the risk

$$RRA = 0.30 - \frac{(0.20)^2}{2} = 0.30 - 0.02 = 0.28$$

standard deviation) is estimated at 0.20. Plugging these values into our formula, we get:

The risk-adjusted return drops from 30% to 28%, accounting for potential volatility. While his might seem minor, understanding the precise impact of risk can reveal if the nvestment aligns with broader strategic objectives.

Application and Analysis

RRAM is especially valuable when assessing opportunities with substantial financial stakes, such as new market entries, strategic partnerships, or high-budget campaigns. By ncorporating risk into growth projections, leaders can make more informed decisions and pursue exponential growth while maintaining a manageable risk profile. This model doesn't discourage risk—it embraces it but requires that risks are evaluated with rigor and responsibility, ensuring calculated, data-backed decisions.

3. THE SUSTAINABLE SCALING FRAMEWORK (SSF)

Once exponential growth is within reach, the next challenge is sustaining it. The Sustainable Scaling Framework (SSF) serves as a roadmap for maintaining momentum and avoiding the pitfalls of unsustainable scaling, which can lead to rapid burnout, resource exhaustion, or even collapse. SSF uses a formula to establish a healthy growth rate that can be sustained without depleting resources.

Core Concept: Growth Sustainability Index

SSF introduces the Growth Sustainability Index (GSI), a metric that evaluates the optimal

$$GSI = \frac{C \times E}{D}$$

growth rate based on the organization's capacity. The GSI formula is as follows:

Where:

- **GSIGSIGSI** = Growth Sustainability Index
- **CCC** = Company's available capacity (such as production capacity, workforce size, etc.)
- **EEE** = Efficiency of resources (a measure of how effectively resources are used)
- **DDD** = Demand pressure (the level of demand or sales pressure on the system)

For instance, let's assume your company has a production capacity of 100 units per day (**C = 100**) and is operating at an efficiency level of 80% (**E = 0.80**). If current demand is at 200

$$GSI = \frac{100 \times 0.80}{200} = \frac{80}{200} = 0.4$$

units per day (**D = 200**), the GSI calculation would be:

In this case, a GSI below 1 indicates that the company is operating at an unsustainable growth rate, unable to meet demand with existing capacity. To achieve sustainability, either capacity or efficiency must increase, or demand must be strategically managed.

Application and Analysis

SSF is crucial for businesses that experience rapid growth but face constraints in resources, workforce, or infrastructure. The GSI provides a clear indication of when scaling up would strain current operations or reduce quality. This model guides leaders in making decisions about resource allocation, hiring, or infrastructure expansion to ensure that growth remains manageable and sustainable.

The SSF Projection

Using SSF, companies can project their GSI over different growth scenarios, helping them decide whether to expand capacity, increase efficiency, or manage demand. By doing so, they position themselves to sustain growth in the long term without risking burnout or diminishing returns.

The journey to exponential growth is not for the faint of heart. But with these three models—EGPM, RRAM, and SSF—you have the tools needed to navigate this challenging but rewarding path. The Exponential Growth Projection Model provides a realistic view of what exponential growth looks like and the compounded power of small, consistent increases. The Risk-Return Analysis Model empowers you to make breakthrough decisions with eyes wide open, understanding the inherent risks. Finally, the Sustainable Scaling Framework ensures that growth, once achieved, remains viable and sustainable.

Each model is a compass, guiding you through the various phases of high-impact growth. Whether you are a startup founder eager to disrupt the market, a seasoned executive managing large-scale operations, or an entrepreneur looking to take your business to the next level, these frameworks offer insights and practical steps to make exponential growth not just a target but a tangible reality.

To truly succeed in creating quantum leaps, these models should not be static tools but dynamic guides—revisited, recalculated, and adapted as conditions evolve. In doing so, you will be better equipped to handle the complexities of high-impact decision-making and, ultimately, to transform ambitious visions into thriving realities. Embrace these tools, and let them serve as the building blocks for your next quantum leap.

Model	Main Formula	Key Variables	Purpose	Example
Exponential Growth Projection Model (EGPM)	$G - P \times (1 + r)^t$	- G: Projected growth value - P: Initial value - r: Growth rate - t: Number of periods	Project compounded growth over time to visualize impact of growth rate	If $P - 1000$ users and $r - 0.15$ monthly, after 12 months $G \approx 5350$ users.
Risk-Return Analysis Model (RRAM)	$RRA - E(R) - \frac{\sigma^2}{2}$	- RRA: Risk-adjusted return - $E(R)$: Expected return - σ: Standard deviation (risk)	Assess whether the expected return on an investment compensates for the associated risk	If $E(R) - 0.30$ and $\sigma - 0.20$, the risk-adjusted return $RRA - 0.28$.
Sustainable Scaling Framework (SSF)	$GSI - \frac{C \times E}{D}$	- GSI: Growth Sustainability Index - C: Available capacity - E: Efficiency - D: Demand	Measure if the growth rate is sustainable or if capacity or efficiency adjustments are needed	If $C - 100$, $E - 0.80$, and $D - 200$, then $GSI - 0.4$ (indicating unsustainable growth).

1. Peter Drucker on Growth and Change

"If you want something new, you have to stop doing something old." — *Peter Drucker*

Applicability: Drucker's insight resonates deeply with the principle behind the Exponential Growth Projection Model (EGPM). Achieving exponential growth often demands breaking away from traditional, linear growth tactics and embracing innovative, high-impact strategies. This perspective reminds leaders that to reach new levels, they must make a conscious shift away from familiar but limiting practices, adapting instead to dynamic approaches that prioritize compounding gains and proactive change.

2. Warren Buffett on Risk and Reward

"Risk comes from not knowing what you're doing." — *Warren Buffett*

Applicability: Buffett's perspective is a cornerstone of the Risk-Return Analysis Model (RRAM). His quote underscores the importance of informed decision-making, where risk is managed through knowledge, preparation, and strategic assessment. In the context of exponential growth, it highlights that understanding the factors at play—such as market conditions, volatility, and opportunity costs—enables businesses to take calculated risks that are justified by potential returns, fostering a balanced approach to breakthrough decisions.

---

3. Albert Einstein on Sustainability and Growth

"We cannot solve our problems with the same thinking we used when we created them." — *Albert Einstein*

Applicability: This reflection by Einstein is pivotal to the Sustainable Scaling Framework (SSF). As companies expand, sustainability becomes a critical focus, requiring fresh perspectives on capacity, efficiency, and demand. Einstein's quote encourages leaders to approach growth with adaptability, innovating in how they manage resources and scaling thoughtfully to maintain long-term viability. It is a reminder that, especially with exponential growth, sustaining success demands evolving our strategies to meet the complexities of each new stage.

CHAPTER 4: THE POWER OF RISK—WHY SMALL STEPS JUST WON'T CUT IT IN THE QUANTUM AGE

"*If you're not willing to risk the unusual, you will have to settle for the ordinary."* — *Jim Rohn*

In this chapter, we tackle a paradox that defines our quantum age: the conventional path to security is the most dangerous route you can take. Today, incremental growth isn't just outdated—it's actively hazardous to your future. Exponential growth, which once seemed risky, is now the safest bet, and the data doesn't lie.

The Myth of Playing It Safe

For decades, businesses and individuals alike were taught that security lies in gradual progress. One cautious step after another. But in the last decade alone, the companies embracing exponential leaps have grown more than 15 times faster than those that play it safe, according to a 2022 study by McKinsey & Company. Companies in the top 10% of risk-takers experienced revenue growth at a staggering 20% compound annual rate, compared to the average of just 3% for those that stuck to incremental improvements.

Why? Because in an age defined by rapid technological advancement and shifting markets, businesses that don't embrace bold change simply get left behind. Just look at Kodak, Nokia, Blockbuster—all once giants, now cautionary tales.

The Quantum Leap Explained

Quantum leaps aren't just a trendy phrase; they're a scientific concept. In physics, quantum leaps represent sudden, massive shifts that redefine the status quo. Electrons jump from one energy level to another without moving through the space in between—an idea that's as powerful as it is perplexing. Imagine the implications of adopting this mindset in your decision-making.

When companies like Netflix, Amazon, and Tesla leapt ahead, they didn't do it by taking incremental steps. They jumped—decisively, boldly, and with the willingness to risk failure. Their success wasn't a result of a perfect roadmap; it was an unyielding commitment to leap into the unknown.

Why We're Wired for Risk Aversion

So, why don't more people and businesses take leaps? Our brains are evolutionarily primed to favor caution. Research from the National Institute of Mental Health shows that the human brain is wired to avoid risk, with fear-based neural circuits firing up even before a real threat exists. Our minds evolved to avoid risks that once meant life or death, but today it's our tolerance for stagnation that might endanger us.

Case in Point: The Tech Giants

Let's dig into some figures to see what quantum decision-making looks like in practice:

1. **Amazon**: In 1997, Amazon was a $16 million online bookstore. But Jeff Bezos didn't stick to that market; he expanded into electronics, music, clothing, cloud computing, and more, even as his advisors warned against it. Today, Amazon generates over $500 billion in annual revenue. The quantum leap approach not only built the world's largest online marketplace but a leader in cloud technology.

2. **Tesla**: When Elon Musk invested in Tesla, electric vehicles were seen as a niche market. Traditional automakers were cautious, producing hybrid cars at best. But Musk bet everything on the full electrification of vehicles, a leap that left competitors scrambling to keep up. As of 2023, Tesla's market cap was greater than the next nine largest automakers combined.

3. **Netflix**: Reed Hastings didn't just move from DVDs to streaming—he made a bet on original content, which put Netflix in direct competition with established studios. This leap from distributor to content creator transformed Netflix into a global entertainment leader, boasting over 238 million subscribers worldwide as of the latest data.

The Decision Matrix for Exponential Growth

But how do you know when it's time to make a quantum leap? This isn't a call to recklessness; it's about calculated, informed risk-taking. Here's a framework that's helped some of today's most successful companies, and it can help you too:

1. **Visionary Leadership**: Leaders need a clear and compelling vision of the future that goes beyond profit. Why does your company exist? What unique value will you add to the world in the next 5, 10, or 50 years?

2. **Market Timing**: Use data to assess if the timing is right. Are market conditions volatile? Are there technological advances or societal shifts that would support this leap?

3. **Adaptive Mindset**: Be ready to pivot based on real-world results. Quantum leaps require flexibility, constant iteration, and learning.

4. **Empowered Teams**: Innovation isn't just about a single leader's vision. Invest in a team that's as excited about the leap as you are—people who understand the power of taking risks for exponential reward.

The New Metrics of Success

Traditional performance indicators—like year-over-year growth, customer retention, and employee satisfaction—are essential but insufficient. Businesses seeking quantum leaps must adopt a new set of KPIs that track potential, adaptability, and reach.

Here are some forward-looking metrics that have shown relevance in recent studies:

- **Disruptive Innovation Index (DII)**: This measures a company's contribution to reshaping an industry. Google, with its AI and machine learning advances, ranks among the top in this metric, while others lag far behind.
- **Agility Rate**: How quickly can your team adjust to new information, market changes, or unexpected challenges? Harvard Business Review finds that companies with high agility rates are 3.5 times more likely to succeed in the long term.
- **Exponential Revenue Multipliers (ERM)**: Instead of measuring by quarter, assess your growth by decade. Where could you be in ten years if you were to leap now?

Embracing Quantum Uncertainty

As you navigate your own leap, remember: uncertainty is your ally, not your enemy. The unknown, which our ancestors feared, is where the most significant breakthroughs await.

Consider This Challenge

Look at the initiatives on your table today and ask yourself: *Is this an incremental step or a quantum leap?* If it's the former, are you content with staying on the safe side of history? Embracing exponential growth might not feel comfortable. In fact, it's likely to feel exactly the opposite. But as the data has shown, inaction and incrementalism come with the highest risk of all.

Are you ready to take the leap? This chapter is your invitation to explore how bold, unconventional moves lead to the most extraordinary transformations.

The Power of Risk—Why Small Steps Just Won't Cut It in the Quantum Age

Rewiring for Quantum Growth

In today's rapidly changing world, the choice is stark: adapt at exponential rates or risk irrelevance. Incremental growth has its merits, but in the age of disruption, it no longer guarantees success. As we venture into this fourth chapter, we'll uncover powerful strategies, models, and tools to help entrepreneurs cultivate a mindset and infrastructure conducive to quantum leaps. These are not simply minor adjustments; they're the bold, paradigm-shifting moves required to thrive in an era where change is the only constant.

Part I: The Power of Quantum Thinking in Business

The essence of quantum leaps in business is rooted in exponential rather than linear thinking. In physics, a quantum leap represents a sudden and significant change in energy levels, skipping incremental steps altogether. Companies and individuals who can harness this mindset are positioned not only to succeed but to redefine their industries.

Defining Quantum Thinking

Quantum thinking challenges traditional risk aversion by asking leaders to visualize the grandest version of their vision and make the bold moves necessary to actualize it. This approach emphasizes:

- **Radical Vision**: A powerful future state that doesn't just improve upon the current but reimagines it.
- **Calculated Risks**: Making moves based on data and market timing, recognizing that not all risks are reckless.
- **Non-linear Growth**: The goal is not gradual improvement but disruptive innovation that leaves competitors behind.

Example: SpaceX entered the heavily regulated and costly aerospace industry with an audacious goal: to reduce the cost of space travel by reusing rockets, a feat never achieved before. Through quantum thinking, SpaceX became the first private company to send humans to the International Space Station, redefining the limits of the space industry.

Part II: Core Models for Quantum Decision-Making

Successful quantum leaps require more than bold aspirations; they require the strategic application of data, adaptability, and team alignment. Here are three models that have empowered exponential growth among leading innovators.

1. The Exponential Growth Model (EGM)

The Exponential Growth Model emphasizes the importance of scalability and compounding growth over time. Unlike traditional models focusing on year-over-year growth, EGM advocates for a vision that projects years or even decades into the future, leveraging technology, market insights, and strategic risk-taking to achieve outsized results.

Key Principles:

- **Compounding Impact**: Each strategic decision should feed into the next, creating a ripple effect that multiplies impact.
- **Innovative Infrastructure**: Build a tech- and data-oriented infrastructure to support rapid expansion.
- **Leveraging Technology**: Automation, artificial intelligence, and digital tools are the backbone of EGM.

Example: Amazon, which began as an online bookstore, used EGM to expand into various industries, including cloud computing and entertainment, by capitalizing on its scalable logistics and technology. Today, Amazon Web Services (AWS) generates nearly half of the company's operating income.

---

2. The Blue Ocean Strategy

This model, created by W. Chan Kim and Renée Mauborgne, encourages companies to escape the confines of traditional competition (red oceans) by creating entirely new markets (blue oceans). This approach involves innovation, understanding customer pain points, and delivering new value.

Key Principles:

- **Value Innovation**: Combine high value with low cost, breaking free from conventional trade-offs.

- **Non-competitive Markets**: Target unmet needs or overlooked markets.
- **Cost and Differentiation Synergy**: Simultaneously focus on lowering costs while improving differentiation.

Case Study: Nintendo's Wii entered the gaming industry with unique motion-control technology that attracted a new demographic of casual gamers, creating a blue ocean. By avoiding direct competition with Xbox and PlayStation, the Wii sold over 100 million units, becoming one of Nintendo's best-selling consoles.

3. The Disruptive Innovation Theory

Introduced by Clayton Christensen, this theory explains how small firms with fewer resources can successfully challenge established companies by targeting overlooked customer segments. Disruptive innovation typically starts by offering simpler, more affordable products or services, evolving into solutions that meet the needs of mainstream consumers.

Key Principles:
- **Targeting Underserved Markets**: Focus on markets or segments that incumbents overlook.
- **Scalability and Adaptability**: Create solutions that can evolve to meet mainstream needs.
- **Incremental Innovation for Radical Change**: Start with smaller innovations that can quickly scale.

Case Study: Netflix began as a DVD rental service for niche users but disrupted the entertainment industry by evolving into a streaming giant and content producer, challenging traditional cable and film production.

Part III: Practical Advice for Entrepreneurs Embracing Quantum Growth

Transitioning from incremental to exponential growth requires a clear strategy, but it also demands a mindset shift for both leaders and teams. Here are actionable steps for the entrepreneur looking to embrace a quantum growth mindset.

1. Cultivate a Risk-Tolerant Culture

Companies that successfully make quantum leaps foster an environment where failure is viewed as a learning opportunity rather than a setback. Risk-tolerant cultures celebrate calculated risk-taking and iterative experimentation.
- **Encourage Experimentation**: Set up a framework for testing and learning from small pilots. Empower teams to innovate and give them the freedom to make bold moves without fear of reprisal.
- **Lead by Example**: Show your team that you're committed to taking risks. Share stories of past failures and the lessons learned, creating an atmosphere of psychological safety.

2. Make Data-Driven Decisions, but Embrace the Unknown

While data is critical, the quantum leap often involves taking steps that data alone cannot justify. Recognize patterns and use predictive analytics to inform strategy, but be willing to go beyond the numbers when the potential for breakthrough innovation exists.

- **Data as a Compass, Not a Map**: Use data to guide, but don't let it limit your vision.
- **Invest in Predictive Tools**: Advanced analytics, AI, and machine learning can reveal insights into customer behavior, market trends, and potential areas for disruption.

3. Develop a Flexible Business Model

Quantum growth demands agility. Developing a flexible business model allows you to pivot quickly and capitalize on emerging opportunities.

- **Continuous Iteration**: Regularly test your business model to ensure it remains relevant. This can involve updating product lines, revising marketing strategies, or pivoting in response to new market demands.
- **Revenue Model Innovation**: Consider subscription services, product bundles, or entirely new monetization methods to increase revenue streams and customer engagement.

Part IV: Key Takeaways and Action Steps

Here, we summarize the core principles of quantum growth and actionable steps to integrate them into your business strategy.

Model	Core Principles	Example
Exponential Growth Model (EGM)	Focus on scalability, tech-driven infrastructure, and compounding impact	Amazon's expansion from books to AWS, logistics, and beyond
Blue Ocean Strategy	Create new markets by targeting unmet needs	Nintendo's Wii, capturing a market of casual gamers
Disruptive Innovation Theory	Begin with overlooked markets, scale to mainstream	Netflix's rise from niche DVD rentals to streaming giant

Key Steps for Leaders

- **Embrace Radical Vision**: Focus on what your business could look like in a future unrestrained by today's limitations.
- **Create a Risk-Tolerant Culture**: Encourage bold experimentation and learn from failure.
- **Leverage Predictive Data, But Stay Bold**: Use data to guide while remaining open to intuitive, visionary decisions.
- **Innovate Your Business Model**: Keep evolving revenue streams and customer engagement strategies.

As you navigate this quantum age, remember that the most transformative moments often come when you step away from traditional models and embrace disruptive potential. Tesla, Amazon, and Netflix didn't succeed by staying in their lanes—they leaped, challenged norms, and took risks that redefined their industries. Now, the next leap could be yours.

Model	Opportunities	Threats	Statistics & Case Studies
Exponential Growth Model (EGM)	- Potential for compound growth rates - High scalability with tech integration - Competitive advantage through rapid innovation	- High costs associated with infrastructure - Risk of market oversaturation - Dependence on emerging tech stability	**Amazon**: Expanded from online retail to cloud computing with AWS, achieving a **10-year CAGR of ~20%**, generating over **$500 billion in annual revenue**.
Blue Ocean Strategy	- Create uncontested market space - Reduced competition - Opportunity for high-profit margins	- Limited data in unexplored markets - Potential misalignment with customer needs - High initial investment	**Nintendo Wii**: Successfully captured the casual gaming market, selling **over 100 million units** by targeting a new audience with unique motion-based gameplay.
Disruptive Innovation Theory	- Capture underserved markets - Low initial competition - Scalability to mainstream markets	- Resistance from established players - Slow initial adoption rates - Regulatory challenges	**Netflix**: Transitioned from niche DVD rentals to a streaming service, now with over **238 million subscribers**, challenging traditional media and cable industries.

CHAPTER 5: THE POWER OF BOLD CHOICES – UNLEASHING THE POTENTIAL OF STRATEGIC DECISIONS

*A*re you making choices that merely sustain your business, or are you daring enough to make the quantum leaps that redefine your growth? What are you willing to sacrifice to reach exponential success? Are you playing it safe, or are you making choices that align with your grandest vision?

These questions aren't just about ambition—they're about survival in an ever-evolving, hyper-competitive market. The decisions that create massive growth often look vastly different from the ones that maintain steady progress. In this chapter, we'll explore the core of breakthrough decision-making, the kind that does not simply move the needle but transforms the very fabric of your business.

The key here is learning to distinguish between decisions that serve the present and those that anticipate a more significant, long-term transformation. It's about seeing beyond the obvious, peering into the potential of what *could be*, and understanding that the exponential growth you seek demands a kind of thinking, courage, and boldness that many avoid out of fear or convenience.

5.1 Identifying the Moments that Define Exponential Growth

Think about the most significant decisions in your life or business thus far. Was there a clear inflection point where a single choice changed everything? Perhaps it was a decision to invest in a new technology, enter an untapped market, or shift your team's culture entirely. Exponential growth doesn't happen by chance; it stems from identifying and seizing pivotal moments that hold the power to multiply your impact.

The question, then, is this: How do you identify these moments with enough clarity and confidence to act decisively? **It begins with recognizing patterns, both within your industry and within your organization, that suggest when a breakthrough opportunity is near.** Patterns might reveal themselves in market trends, disruptive technologies, shifts in consumer behavior, or changes in global economic policies. By learning to spot these patterns and aligning them with your organization's strengths, you'll become adept at recognizing when the time is right to make the kind of bold choice that accelerates growth.

However, recognizing these moments is not enough. You must cultivate an internal readiness to capitalize on them. Many leaders identify growth opportunities yet remain shackled by the fear of failure or the uncertainty of the unknown. True quantum leaps happen when you not only see the opportunity but are prepared to act on it with onviction. This readiness can only come from the deep-rooted understanding that the most significant risks often lead to the most substantial rewards.

5.2 Beyond Incrementalism: The Case for Quantum Leaps

In a world where incremental growth has become the norm, quantum leaps can feel risky, even reckless. But ask yourself: How much time and energy are you willing to invest in incremental growth versus the rewards of exponential scaling? Incremental growth may offer the comfort of predictability, but it often leaves a company trailing behind more daring competitors who are unafraid to embrace the power of transformation.

To illustrate, let's consider the difference between two companies in the same industry— one that seeks to improve its processes by five percent each year, and another that aims to redefine its business model entirely, even at the risk of alienating some of its existing customer base. While the former company might experience slow, predictable growth, the latter is poised for exponential gains because it's willing to take the leaps that redefine the market itself.

Choosing to take quantum leaps does not imply recklessness; it requires a carefully calibrated strategy where bold decisions are made based on research, data, and a deep understanding of market forces. **Exponential growth happens when you combine visionary thinking with analytical precision, aligning each bold choice with your long-term mission and competitive advantage.**

5.3 Making Decisions that Matter: A Framework for Strategic Choices

If making the right choices for exponential growth is essential, then how do we ensure that each decision supports this goal? Developing a framework for decision-making can help guide your team, reduce uncertainty, and increase the likelihood of long-term success. Here's a three-part framework to consider when weighing your options:

1. **Clarity of Vision**: First and foremost, every decision must align with the overall vision for your company. Too many businesses make choices based on short-term gains that detract from their larger objectives. To avoid this, make your vision clear and specific, and let it serve as the compass for every strategic move.

2. **Depth of Research**: Quantum decisions are not based on guesswork; they require thorough investigation. Look at your options, evaluate risks, and use data to support each choice. Consider the implications from multiple angles— financial, cultural, operational—and determine how each choice aligns with both current and future market conditions.

3. **Willingness to Adapt**: The most significant decisions are often made in volatile conditions. To thrive, a business must be agile enough to adapt as new information becomes available. This means not only committing to a choice but staying flexible enough to pivot if the landscape shifts. Adaptability can be the difference between a leap that pays off and one that doesn't.

5.4 Embracing Uncertainty and Building Resilience

At the heart of every bold choice lies a certain degree of uncertainty. The unknown is both terrifying and exhilarating, and the very idea of exponential growth can often feel daunting.

Embracing this uncertainty is crucial. In fact, *the leaders who achieve exponential growth are those who thrive on the unknown,* who see unpredictability not as a threat but as an opportunity to evolve and innovate.

The path to quantum success is seldom linear. Challenges will arise, and setbacks will test your resilience. It is during these moments that a leader's true commitment to exponential growth is tested. Embrace these challenges as learning opportunities, staying focused on the end goal even when the journey is less than ideal. Building resilience isn't about ignoring fear or doubt; it's about acknowledging them and choosing to press on regardless.

The best leaders cultivate a resilient mindset within their teams as well, fostering a culture where failure is seen as a stepping stone to greater success. This perspective, combined with an unwavering commitment to the larger vision, creates an organization capable of weathering the storms and emerging stronger on the other side.

5.5 Aligning Your Team with Bold Decisions

No significant decision can be executed alone. For exponential growth to take hold, your team must not only understand the vision but be fully aligned with the bold choices you make along the way. Clear communication, trust, and transparency are essential here.

Bring your team into the decision-making process early on. Share the why behind each choice, showing them not just what you're doing but what it means for the organization's future. Building a culture where every member feels like a contributor to the vision fosters loyalty and drives the collective momentum needed for quantum growth.

Empower your team to take ownership of their roles in executing these bold decisions. Encourage innovative thinking, reward risk-taking, and create an environment where every employee feels their input matters. The most successful leaders inspire their teams to be proactive partners in achieving exponential growth, turning a singular vision into a shared mission.

5.6 Celebrating Wins and Learning from Losses

Exponential growth, while exhilarating, can be exhausting. To maintain momentum, take the time to celebrate milestones, both big and small. Recognizing and rewarding achievements reinforces the commitment to the vision and helps sustain motivation, even when the path forward becomes challenging.

Simultaneously, it's equally important to review decisions that didn't pan out as expected. Growth comes from learning, and every setback is a lesson in resilience and adaptability. Approach these moments with a growth mindset, analyzing them to refine future strategies and build an even stronger foundation for the leaps to come.

Your Quantum Leap Awaits

The power of bold choices lies in their ability to shift the trajectory of your business and redefine what's possible. By embracing quantum leaps, you not only pave the way for exponential growth but inspire those around you to dream bigger, aim higher, and achieve more than they thought possible.

The journey isn't without risk, and the decisions required aren't easy. But by making choices that align with your most audacious goals, building a resilient team, and cultivating a culture of innovation, you set the stage for growth that transcends the limitations of ordinary strategy. **So, ask yourself: Are you ready to make the bold decisions that will propel you toward your quantum leap?**

CHAPTER 6: THE FUTURE'S GREATEST CHALLENGES – ANTICIPATING AND OVERCOMING THE BARRIERS TO EXPONENTIAL GROWTH

*A*s an entrepreneur, are you prepared for the complexities that lie ahead? What if the obstacles you're set to encounter are ones the current marketplace hasn't even fully realized? How will you position yourself and your company to not only survive but thrive in an unpredictable future?

Entrepreneurship has always involved risk and ingenuity, but as technology advances at a dizzying pace and global dynamics evolve, future entrepreneurs will face challenges that are unprecedented in their scope and complexity. Understanding these potential roadblocks will empower you to anticipate, adapt, and make the kind of breakthrough decisions that foster resilience and sustained growth. In this chapter, we'll explore five pressing issues that entrepreneurs will likely encounter in the future and how they might prepare to tackle them head-on.

6.1 Problematic 1: Navigating Rapid Technological Advancements

The pace of technological change is accelerating, impacting every aspect of business—from production and logistics to customer service and data analysis. But with this surge in innovation comes the daunting task of staying ahead of the curve. For future entrepreneurs, keeping up with technological advancements won't simply mean adopting the latest tools or software; it will mean continuously transforming how they operate, interact with customers, and innovate within their industries.

For instance, emerging technologies like artificial intelligence, blockchain, quantum computing, and IoT (Internet of Things) offer immense potential but demand specialized knowledge and substantial investment. The challenge lies not only in understanding and implementing these technologies but also in predicting which ones will become foundational versus which will be transient. **Future entrepreneurs must develop an acute sense for technological trends, honing the ability to distinguish between fleeting fads and game-changing advancements.**

Moreover, with new technology comes the risk of obsolescence. Companies that fail to adapt quickly may find their offerings outdated, their processes inefficient, and their competitive edge lost to more agile players. Entrepreneurs of the future must cultivate a mindset of continuous learning and strategic agility, preparing their organizations to pivot and reorient as technology evolves. This requires not just a commitment to innovation but a willingness to reassess and recalibrate at every step of the journey.

2 Problematic 2: Addressing Workforce Automation and Human Capital Challenges

Automation and AI are already transforming workplaces, and this trend is only set to accelerate. As more tasks become automated, entrepreneurs will face a dual challenge: managing the transition to automation while preserving human capital and cultivating a culture of innovation and adaptability. The future workforce will look dramatically different, with a stronger emphasis on skills like creativity, emotional intelligence, and critical thinking—qualities that machines are far from mastering.

The challenge here lies in striking a balance between efficiency and empathy. Automation promises significant cost savings and operational efficiency, but it also threatens to disrupt entire categories of jobs, creating workforce instability and potentially eroding employee morale. Future entrepreneurs must be prepared to manage these tensions, creating workplaces where technology and human talent coexist harmoniously.

This challenge will demand a new approach to workforce development, where continuous upskilling and reskilling become the norm. Entrepreneurs who want to stay competitive will need to invest in training programs that empower employees to evolve alongside technology. Additionally, they'll need to foster a culture that values human contribution, innovation, and adaptability, ensuring that the human element remains a central pillar of the organization. In the future, companies that successfully integrate automation without sacrificing the essence of their workforce will be the ones that thrive.

3 Problematic 3: Maintaining Data Privacy and Cybersecurity in a Digital World

With the digitalization of business operations comes an increased reliance on data—customer data, market analytics, employee information, and more. While data is a powerful asset, it also brings substantial risks. In the future, data privacy and cybersecurity will be paramount concerns for entrepreneurs, not only due to the potential financial losses associated with breaches but also due to the erosion of consumer trust that can result from mishandling sensitive information.

As regulations surrounding data privacy become more stringent globally, entrepreneurs will be held to higher standards, and failure to comply could result in costly penalties and reputational damage. Future entrepreneurs must be proactive in developing robust data governance policies, ensuring that customer data is handled with the utmost care and that the organization is compliant with evolving legal frameworks. **Cybersecurity strategies will need to be dynamic, evolving to meet increasingly sophisticated threats in real-time.**

But beyond technical measures, cybersecurity will also require a cultural shift within organizations. Employees at every level must be educated on data privacy best practices, as even a single error or lapse in judgment can lead to a breach. Entrepreneurs will face the challenge of building a culture of vigilance and accountability, where every team member understands the importance of data security and plays an active role in safeguarding it. The businesses that earn consumer trust by demonstrating their commitment to data privacy will likely have a distinct advantage in the years to come.

5.4 Problematic 4: Adapting to Environmental and Social Responsibility Demands

Today's consumers are more socially and environmentally conscious than ever, and this trend will only intensify. Entrepreneurs of the future will face mounting pressure to demonstrate their commitment to sustainability, ethical sourcing, and corporate responsibility. Businesses that fail to meet these expectations may find themselves losing customers to more conscientious competitors, regardless of the quality or price of their products.

This challenge goes beyond adopting environmentally friendly practices or donating to charitable causes. **It's about integrating social and environmental responsibility into the core of the business model**—from sustainable supply chains to ethical labor practice and environmentally conscious production methods. Future entrepreneurs must recogniz that their actions have far-reaching implications and that consumers are increasingly holding companies accountable for their impact on the world.

Incorporating these values requires a commitment to transparency. Consumers want to know not just that companies are taking action but how they're making a difference. This means providing detailed, accessible information about sustainability initiatives and holding the business accountable for meeting its goals. It's a complex undertaking, as it ma demand a complete overhaul of traditional business practices, often at a higher cost. Yet th companies that succeed in aligning profitability with purpose will not only attract loyal customers but also build resilient brands capable of thriving in a world that increasingly values ethics over convenience.

6.5 Problematic 5: Coping with Global Market Volatility and Economic Uncertainty

As globalization continues to blur traditional borders, entrepreneurs of the future will operate in an increasingly interconnected—and volatile—marketplace. The impacts of events like global pandemics, geopolitical tensions, trade wars, and climate-related disasters have demonstrated the unpredictability of the global economy, and future entrepreneurs will need to be prepared for these disruptions.

This will require a heightened focus on adaptability and risk management. Entrepreneurs will need to develop business models that are resilient to external shocks and flexible enough to pivot in response to sudden changes in the market. **A key challenge will be building a diversified portfolio of revenue streams, suppliers, and markets, ensuring that the business isn't overly reliant on any single source.** For example, a company tha relies solely on international suppliers may be vulnerable to trade disruptions, whereas a business that diversifies its supplier base can weather these challenges more effectively.

Additionally, future entrepreneurs will need to navigate the complexities of operating in different regulatory environments. As countries introduce new trade regulations, taxes, and tariffs, companies must be agile enough to adjust pricing, sourcing, and market strategies accordingly. This demands not only a deep understanding of global economics but also a capacity for strategic foresight and scenario planning.

While this volatility presents risks, it also offers opportunities. Entrepreneurs who learn to thrive in uncertain conditions will have the advantage, as they can identify emerging trends and unmet needs that arise from these shifts. The future will reward those who can turn challenges into opportunities, leveraging agility and insight to stay ahead in an unpredictable world.

Preparing for the Future

The challenges facing future entrepreneurs are daunting, but they are not insurmountable. By understanding these obstacles and proactively developing strategies to address them, you can position yourself and your business for long-term success.

Staying ahead in an era of rapid technological change, balancing automation with human capital, prioritizing data privacy, integrating sustainability, and managing global volatility—these are the essential competencies that will define the most successful entrepreneurs of tomorrow. Each of these challenges is an opportunity to stand out, differentiate your brand, and create value in ways that are both innovative and resilient.

As we move forward into an era where exponential growth is both a possibility and a necessity, it's the entrepreneurs who tackle these issues with creativity, foresight, and adaptability who will make the greatest impact. So, the question remains: Are you prepared to embrace these challenges, make the bold choices required, and position yourself as a leader in the future of entrepreneurship?

APPENDICES

Purpose: To give you a clear, actionable framework for making high-impact decisions that set the stage for exponential growth.

Sections:

1. **Identifying Key Decision Areas**
   Start by asking: Where do I most need a breakthrough? Think about areas where you feel stuck, where competition is intense, or where opportunity seems untapped. Use these questions to guide you:
   - Which areas of my business (or life) need a fresh perspective?
   - Where am I facing repeated challenges or bottlenecks?
   - What new ideas or opportunities excite me the most?

2. **Evaluating Decision Options**
   Not all options lead to exponential growth. Evaluate each potential decision using these criteria:
   - **Risk-Reward Balance**: Is the potential reward worth the risk?
   - **Alignment with Vision**: Does this decision bring me closer to my long-term vision?
   - **Scalability**: Does this choice open doors to scale my growth?

3. **Framework for Risk Mitigation**
   Breakthrough decisions are bold, but they don't need to be reckless. Use this checklist to assess and mitigate risks:
   - Identify potential risks associated with each decision.
   - Prioritize risks from "most likely" to "least likely."
   - Develop mitigation strategies for top risks (for instance, backup plans or phased implementation).

4. **Action Steps for Implementation**
   Once you've made your decision, turn it into action with this template:
   - **Milestones**: Define major steps and key deadlines.
   - **Accountability**: Assign tasks and responsibilities.
   - **Impact Tracking**: Set metrics to measure progress.

Appendix B: Tools for Exponential Growth

Purpose: Explore cutting-edge tools, techniques, and insights to fuel your journey to exponential growth.

Sections:

1. **Mindset and Mental Models**
   Developing a quantum leap mindset begins with how you see the world. Here are key mental models to adopt:
   - **First Principles Thinking**: Break complex problems down to their basics and build solutions from scratch.
   - **10X Thinking**: Aim for 10X improvement over incremental gains. Ask, "What would I need to do differently to reach 10X growth?"

2. **Digital Tools and Software**
   Leverage technology to supercharge growth. Explore these recommended tools:
   - **Project Management**: Tools like Asana or Trello help manage complex projects.
   - **Collaboration**: Platforms like Slack or Microsoft Teams enhance communication and teamwork.
   - **Automation**: Zapier and Integromat can automate repetitive tasks, freeing up time for strategic work.

3. **Performance Metrics**
   Knowing what to measure is key to growth. Track these essential KPIs:
   - **Customer Satisfaction**: Net Promoter Score (NPS) and Customer Effort Score (CES).
   - **Operational Efficiency**: Measure cost savings, process completion times, or error rates.
   - **Growth Rate**: Monitor revenue growth, customer acquisition, or market share.

4. **Resource Libraries**
   Dive deeper into growth strategies with these resources:
   - **Books**: "Good to Great" by Jim Collins, "The Lean Startup" by Eric Ries.
   - **Courses**: Online learning platforms like Coursera or Udemy offer specialized courses on leadership and strategy.
   - **Articles**: Industry journals and sites like Harvard Business Review or McKinsey Insights.

Appendix C: Case Studies and Examples of Quantum Leaps

Purpose: Inspire your own breakthroughs by learning from bold decisions that led to transformative growth.

Sections:

1. **Industry-Specific Quantum Leaps**
   See how leaders from different industries made big leaps:
   - **Technology**: How a shift to a cloud-based model transformed Netflix into a streaming powerhouse.
   - **Healthcare**: How telemedicine redefined accessibility and healthcare delivery.

2. **Entrepreneurial Success Stories**
   Real entrepreneurs who made audacious moves:
   - **Sara Blakely of Spanx**: From idea to empire by tapping an overlooked need in women's fashion.
   - **Elon Musk of SpaceX**: Revolutionized space travel by aiming for reusable rockets to cut costs.

3. **Lessons Learned**
   What these stories show us:
   - **Take Calculated Risks**: Each leader faced risks but strategically minimized them.
   - **Persist Through Failures**: None of these successes came without setbacks. Learn, adapt, and try again.

4. **Comparative Analysis of Success vs. Failure**
   Analyzing both sides:
   - Successes often come down to timing, innovation, and risk management.
   - Failures often stem from overlooking market needs, ignoring customer feedback, or underestimating costs.

Appendix D: Personal Growth and Leadership Development Exercises

Purpose: Personal growth fuels professional growth. Use these exercises to strengthen your leadership capabilities.

Sections:

1. **Self-Reflection Exercises**
   Start by understanding yourself. Here are a few questions:
   - What values drive my decisions?
   - Where do I feel most confident in my leadership, and where could I improve?
   - How comfortable am I with taking risks?

2. **Leadership Skills Inventory**
   Assess your leadership skills. Rate yourself in areas like:
   - **Communication**: How well do you articulate goals, give feedback, and inspire your team?
   - **Adaptability**: Are you open to change, and do you handle new challenges with ease?
3. **Goal-Setting for Personal and Professional Growth**
   Create bold yet achievable goals with this process:
   - **Vision**: What is your long-term vision?
   - **Milestones**: What steps will you need to take to reach this vision?
   - **Timeline**: Set realistic deadlines to reach each milestone.
4. **Mindfulness and Resilience-Building Techniques**
   Effective leaders stay grounded. Try these techniques:
   - **Mindfulness Meditation**: Spend 10 minutes each day in meditation to reduce stress.
   - **Resilience Journal**: Write down challenges and how you overcame them; this builds confidence in future decision-making.

Appendix E: Quantum Leap Roadmap Template

Purpose: Map out your path to exponential growth with this customizable roadmap template.

Sections:

1. **Goal Definition Worksheet**
   Define clear, impactful goals that align with your vision. Use these prompts:
   - What do I want to achieve in the next 5–10 years?
   - What smaller goals will help me get there?
2. **Strategy Planning Template**
   Break down your strategy into actionable steps:
   - **Short-Term Actions**: Immediate steps to set the groundwork.
   - **Long-Term Actions**: Big moves that push toward exponential growth.
3. **Milestone and Accountability Tracker**
   Keep your momentum by tracking your milestones:
   - **Milestones**: List key achievements.
   - **Review Dates**: Set periodic check-ins to evaluate progress.
4. **Resource Allocation Planning**
   Allocate resources strategically:
   - **Time**: Prioritize time on high-impact activities.
   - **Finances**: Budget for growth-related investments, including technology and personnel.

END

www.ingramcontent.com/pod-product-compliance
Lightning Source LLC
Chambersburg PA
CBHW070135230526
45472CB00004B/1534